Highlights® Handbook

Getting Ready for Phonics

Compiled by Constance McAllister

Pictures by Jerome Weisman, Katharine Dodge, and others

2

aA	bB	cC	dD	eE	fF

apple
acorn | bus | corn celery | duck | egg eagle | fish

nN	oO	pP	qQ	rR	sS	tT

nest

oval
ostrich

pie

question mark

robot

sandwich

table

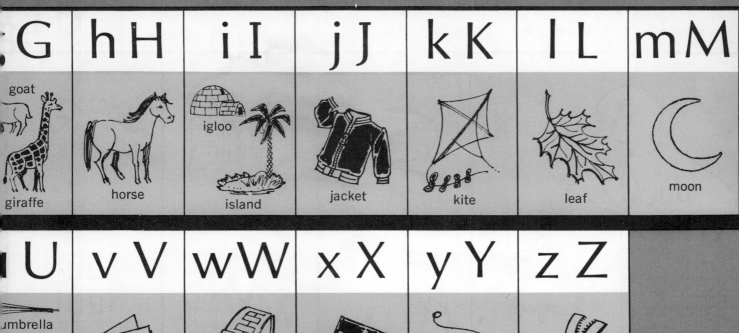

gG	hH	iI	jJ	kK	lL	mM
goat giraffe	horse	igloo island	jacket	kite	leaf	moon

U	vV	wW	xX	yY	zZ

umbrella unicorn | valentine | watch | x-ray | yo-yo | zipper

For each pictured clue, say a word that begins with **d**.

1. d _ _ _

2. d _ _ _

3. d _ _ _ _ _ _

4. d _ _ _

5. d _ _ _

6. d _ _ _ _ _

7. d _ _ _

More Things To Do:

On a piece of paper, write the answers to numbers 1 through 7.
Check your spelling on page 40.

In each box, find the one that is different.

Short Sound of a

Sometimes the letter that we call <u>a</u>
sounds like what we say. . .

at the beginning of apple

the middle of cat

the beginning of anchor

and the middle of hat

Find these little pictures
in the big picture at the right.
These words have the short <u>a</u> sound.

Long Sound of a

Sometimes the letter that we call <u>a</u> sounds like what we say...

at the beginning of apron

the middle of snake

the beginning of acorn

and the middle of cake

Find these little pictures
in the big picture at the right.
These words have the long <u>a</u> sound.

For each pictured clue, say a word that begins with **w**.

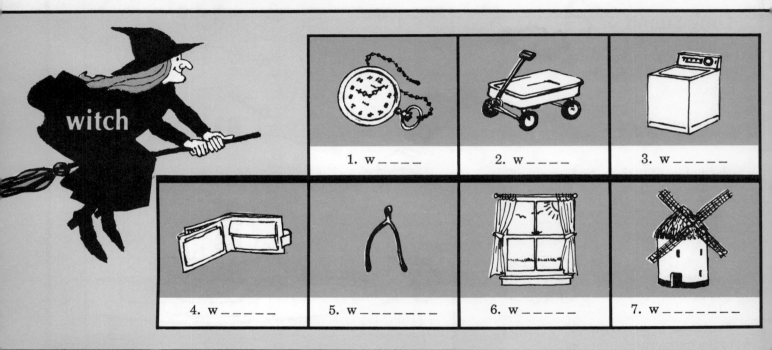

witch

1. w _ _ _ _

2. w _ _ _ _

3. w _ _ _ _ _

4. w _ _ _ _ _

5. w _ _ _ _ _ _

6. w _ _ _ _

7. w _ _ _ _ _ _

More Things To Do:

On a piece of paper, write the answers to numbers 1 through 7.
Check your spelling on page 40.

For each pictured clue, say a word that begins with **f**.

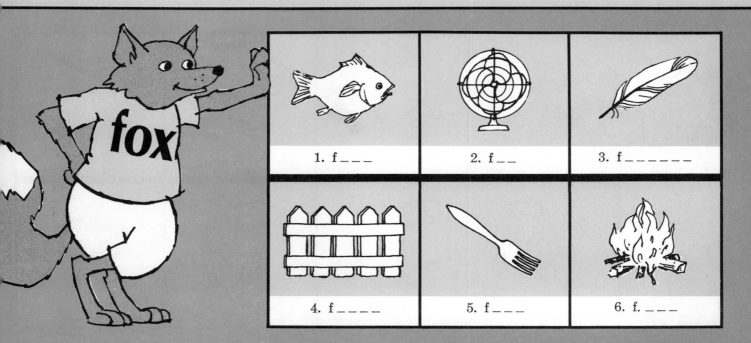

1. f _ _ _
2. f _ _
3. f _ _ _ _ _
4. f _ _ _ _
5. f _ _ _
6. f. _ _ _

More Things To Do:

On a piece of paper, write the answers to numbers 1 through 6.
Check your spelling on page 40.

For each pictured clue, say a word that begins with <u>n</u>.

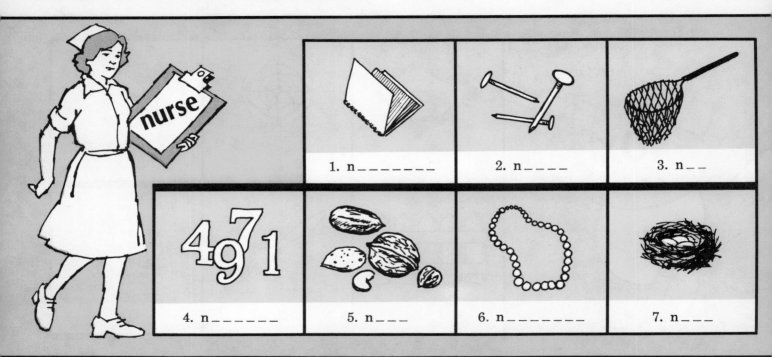

1. n _ _ _ _ _ _

2. n _ _ _ _

3. n _ _

4. n _ _ _ _ _ _

5. n _ _ _

6. n _ _ _ _ _ _

7. n _ _ _

More Things To Do:

On a piece of paper, write the answers to numbers 1 through 7.
Check your spelling on page 40.

aA bB cC dD eE fF gG hH iI jJ kK lL mM

Frank April William Debbie Nicholas

Look at each child's name.
Find below a picture of something that begins with the same letter.

windmill desk frog nickel apron

nN oO pP qQ rR sS tT uU vV wW xX yY zZ

For each pictured clue, say a word that begins with **l**.

1. l _ _ _ _ _ _

2. l _ _ _ _ _

3. l _ _ _

4. l _ _ _

5. l _ _ _

6. l _ _ _ _ _

More Things To Do:

On a piece of paper, write the answers to numbers 1 through 6.
Check your spelling on page 40.

In each box, find the one that is different.

Short Sound of i

The letter **i** is written here;
its short sound is what you hear...

at the beginning of igloo

the middle of king

the beginning of insect

and the middle of ring

Find these little pictures
in the big picture at the right.
These words have the short **i** sound.

Long Sound of i

The letter **i** is written here;
its long sound is what you hear...

at the beginning of ice cream

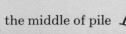

the middle of pile

the beginning of island

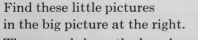

and the middle of smile

Find these little pictures
in the big picture at the right.
These words have the long **i** sound.

For each pictured clue, say a word that begins with **h**.

1. h _ _ _ _

2. h _ _ _ _ _

3. h _ _ _

4. h _ _

5. h _ _ _

6. h _ _ _ _ _ _ _ _ _

More Things To Do:

On a piece of paper, write the answers to numbers 1 through 6.
Check your spelling on page 40.

For each pictured clue, say a word that begins with **m**.

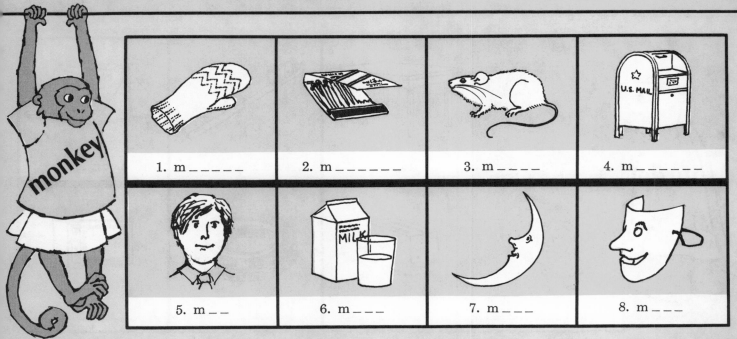

1. m _ _ _ _ _

2. m _ _ _ _ _ _

3. m _ _ _ _

4. m _ _ _ _ _ _

5. m _ _

6. m _ _ _

7. m _ _ _

8. m _ _ _

monkey

More Things To Do:

On a piece of paper, write the answers to numbers 1 through 8.
Check your spelling on page 40.

For each pictured clue, say a word that begins with <u>t</u>.

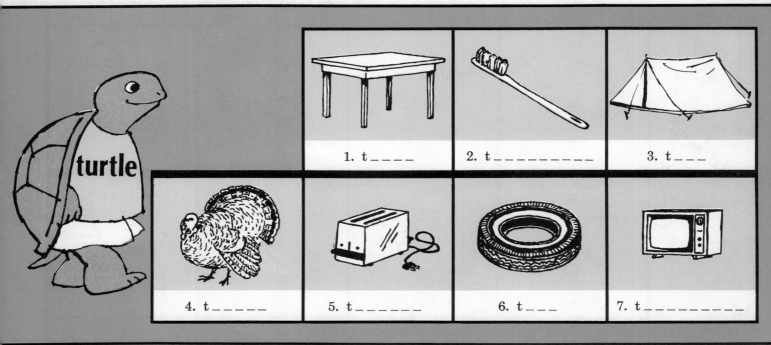

1. t _ _ _ _

2. t _ _ _ _ _ _ _ _ _

3. t _ _ _

4. t _ _ _ _ _

5. t _ _ _ _ _ _

6. t _ _ _

7. t _ _ _ _ _ _ _ _ _

More Things To Do:
On a piece of paper, write the answers to numbers 1 through 7.
Check your spelling on page 40.

aA bB cC dD eE fF gG hH iI jJ kK lL mM

 **Iris**

 **Peter**

 **Tracey**

 **Manuel**

 **Heather**

Look at each child's name.
Find below a picture of something that begins with the same letter.

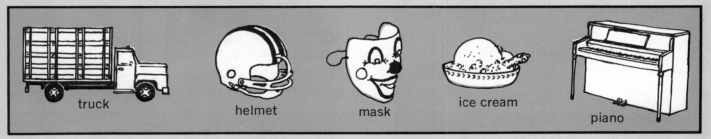

truck helmet mask ice cream piano

nN oO pP qQ rR sS tT uU vV wW xX yY zZ

Short Sound of O

Here is a letter that's fat and round;
listen for the short <u>o</u> sound. . .

at the beginning of ox

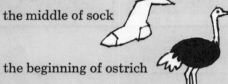

the middle of sock

the beginning of ostrich

and the middle of lock

Find these little pictures
in the big picture at the right.
These words have the short <u>o</u> sound.

Long Sound of O

Here is a letter that's fat and round;
listen for the long <u>o</u> sound. . .

at the beginning of ocean

the middle of goat

the beginning of oval

and the middle of boat

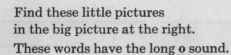

Find these little pictures
in the big picture at the right.
These words have the long <u>o</u> sound.

For each pictured clue, say a word that begins with the letter shown.

x X

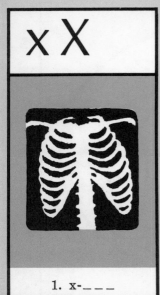

1. x-_ _ _

y Y

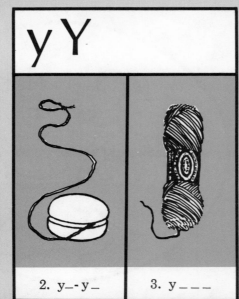

2. y_-y_

3. y_ _ _

z Z

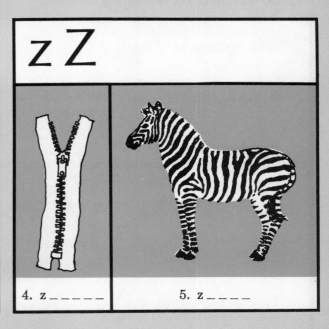

4. z_ _ _ _ _

5. z_ _ _ _

More Things To Do:
On a piece of paper, write the answers to numbers 1 through 5.
Check your spelling on page 40.

In each box, find the one that is different.

For each pictured clue, say a word that begins with **r**.

robot

1. r _ _ _ _ _ _

2. r _ _ _

3. r _ _ _

4. r _ _ _ _

5. r _ _ _ _

6. r _ _ _ _ _

More Things To Do:

On a piece of paper, write the answers to numbers 1 through 6.
Check your spelling on page 40.

For each pictured clue, say a word that begins with **j**.

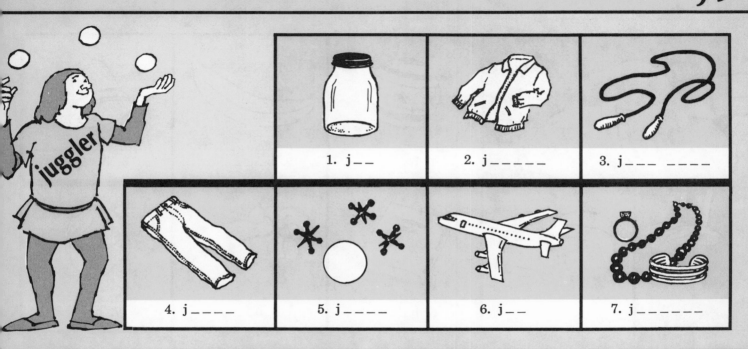

1. j _ _

2. j _ _ _ _ _

3. j _ _ _   _ _ _ _

4. j _ _ _ _

5. j _ _ _ _

6. j _ _

7. j _ _ _ _ _ _

More Things To Do:

On a piece of paper, write the answers to numbers 1 through 7.
Check your spelling on page 40.

For each pictured clue, say a word that begins with **b**.

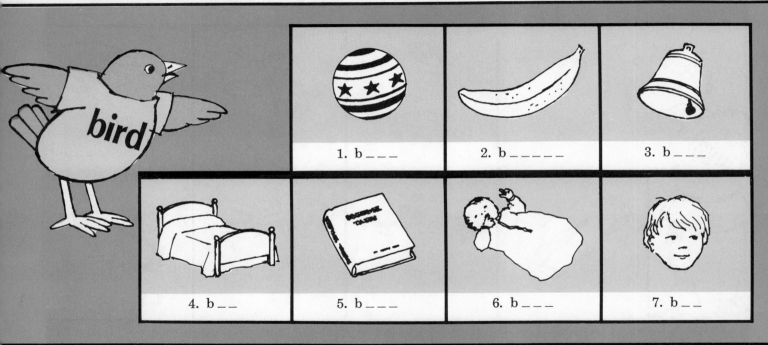

1. b _ _ _

2. b _ _ _ _ _

3. b _ _ _

4. b _ _

5. b _ _ _

6. b _ _ _

7. b _ _

More Things To Do:
On a piece of paper, write the answers to numbers 1 through 7.
Check your spelling on page 40.

a A b B c C d D e E f F g G h H i I j J k K l L m M

Ben   Yolanda   Robert   Janet   Quentin

Look at each child's name.
Find below a picture of something that begins with the same letter.

rocket   jacket   question mark   bell   yo-yo

n N o O p P q Q r R s S t T u U v V w W x X y Y z Z

Short Sound of e

When you see the letter **e**
the sound it makes may be...

like the beginning of egg

the middle of bell

the beginning of elephant

and the middle of shell

Find these little pictures
in the big picture at the right.
These words have the short **e** sound.

Long Sound of e

When you see the letter **e**
the sound it makes may be. . .

like the beginning of eagle

the middle of queen

the beginning of easel

and the middle of bean

Find these little pictures
in the big picture at the right.
These words have the long **e** sound.

v V

For each pictured clue, say a word that begins with **v**.

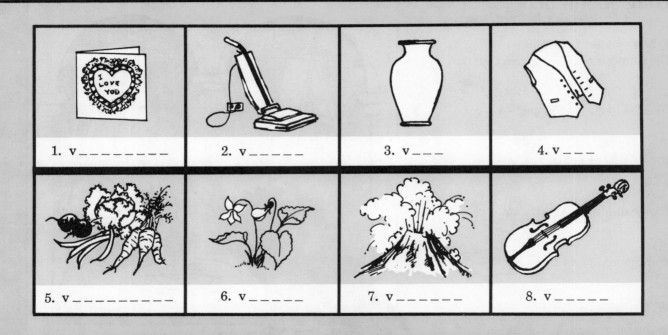

1. v _ _ _ _ _ _ _ _

2. v _ _ _ _ _

3. v _ _ _

4. v _ _ _

5. v _ _ _ _ _ _ _ _ _

6. v _ _ _ _ _

7. v _ _ _ _ _ _

8. v _ _ _ _ _

More Things To Do:

On a piece of paper, write the answers to numbers 1 through 8.
Check your spelling on page 40.

For each pictured clue, say a word that begins with **p**.

penguin

1. p _ _

2. p _ _ _

3. p _ _ _ _ _

4. p _ _ _ _ _ _

5. p _ _ _ _ _

6. p _ _

More Things To Do:

On a piece of paper, write the answers to numbers 1 through 6.
Check your spelling on page 40.

aA bB cC dD eE fF gG hH iI jJ kK lL mM

 **Karen**
 **Robin**
 **Steve**
 **Undine**
 **George**

Look at each child's name.
Find below a picture of something that begins with the same letter.

robot giraffe kangaroo star umbrella

nN oO pP qQ rR sS tT uU vV wW xX yY zZ

In each box, find the one that is different.

B B P	f ſ f
E F E	Y Y v
l t t	M M M
x x ＼	O Q Q

Short Sound of U

Sometimes <u>u</u> will make the sound
that is like what's found. . .

at the beginning of umbrella

the middle of duck

the beginning of up

and the middle of truck

Find these little pictures
in the big picture at the right.
These words have the short <u>u</u> sound.

Long Sound of U

Sometimes <u>u</u> will make the sound
that is like what's found...

at the beginning of unicorn

the middle of bugle

the beginning of uniform

and the middle of mule

Find these little pictures
in the big picture at the right.
These words have the long <u>u</u> sound.

k K

For each pictured clue, say a word that begins with **k**.

1. k _ _ _

2. k _ _ _ _ _ _

3. k _ _

4. k _ _ _

5. k _ _ _

6. k _ _ _ _ _

More Things To Do:

On a piece of paper, write the answers to numbers 1 through 6.
Check your spelling on page 40.

a A b B c C d D e E f F g G h H i I j J k K l L m M

Carol   Edward   Harry   Gail   Leon

Look at each child's name.
Find below a picture of something that begins with the same letter.

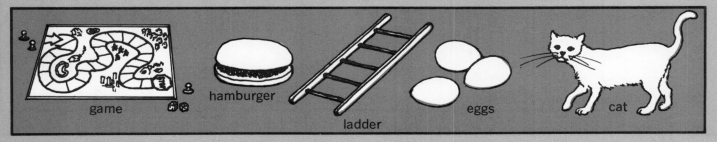

game   hamburger   ladder   eggs   cat

n N o O p P q Q r R s S t T u U v V w W x X y Y z Z

For each pictured clue, say a word that begins with <u>s</u>.

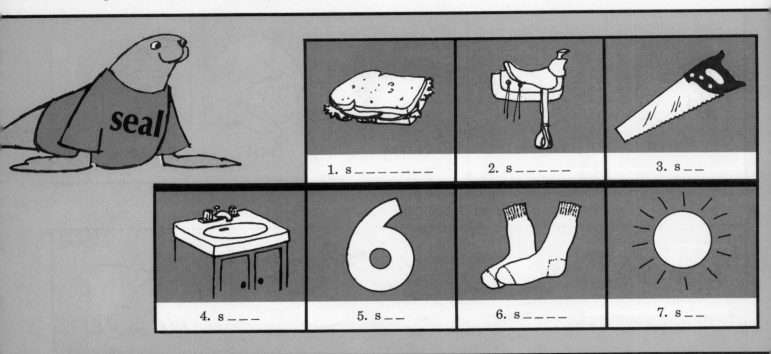

1. s _ _ _ _ _ _ _

2. s _ _ _ _ _

3. s _ _

4. s _ _ _

5. s _ _

6. s _ _ _ _

7. s _ _

More Things To Do:

On a piece of paper, write the answers to numbers 1 through 7.
Check your spelling on page 40.

In each box, find the one that is different.

D D ⊃	W (upside down W) W W	P R R	b b ⊂
e c e	G G G	⊢ F F	N ∧ N

40

Answers

Page 4	1.dish 2.desk 3.dinosaur 4.doll 5.deer 6.doctor 7.door	**Page 22**	1.x-ray 2.yo-yo 3.yarn 4.zipper 5.zebra
Page 8	1.watch 2.wagon 3.washer 4.wallet 5.wishbone 6.window 7.windmill	**Page 24**	1.rooster 2.rope 3.rake 4.ruler 5.radio 6.racket
Page 9	1.fish 2.fan 3.feather 4.fence 5.fork 6.fire	**Page 25**	1.jar 2.jacket 3.jump rope 4.jeans 5.jacks 6.jet 7.jewelry
Page 10	1.notebook 2.nails 3.net 4.numbers 5.nuts 6.necklace 7.nest	**Page 26**	1.ball 2.banana 3.bell 4.bed 5.book 6.baby 7.boy
Page 12	1.lettuce 2.ladder 3.lamp 4.leaf 5.lock 6.lobster	**Page 30**	1.valentine 2.vacuum 3.vase 4.vest 5.vegetables 6.violet 7.volcano 8.vio
Page 16	1.house 2.hammer 3.hose 4.hat 5.hand 6.helicopter	**Page 31**	1.pie 2.pear 3.puzzle 4.pumpkin 5.pencil 6.pig
Page 17	1.mitten 2.matches 3.mouse 4.mailbox 5.man 6.milk 7.moon 8.mask	**Page 36**	1.king 2.kittens 3.key 4.kite 5.kick 6.kettle
Page 18	1.table 2.toothbrush 3.tent 4.turkey 5.toaster 6.tire 7.television	**Page 38**	1.sandwich 2.saddle 3.saw 4.sink 5.six 6.socks 7.sun